Writing for Business Results

Patricia E. Seraydarian, Ph.D.

American Media Publishing
4900 University Avenue
West Des Moines, IA 50266-6769
800-262-2557

Writing for Business Results

Patricia E. Seraydarian, Ph.D.
Copyright ©1996 by Richard D. Irwin, Inc.

This publication is designed to provide accurate and authoritative information in regard to the subject matter covered. It is sold with the understanding that neither the author nor the publisher is engaged in rendering legal, accounting, or other professional service. If legal advice or other expert assistance is required, the services of a competent professional person should be sought.

Credits:

American Media Publishing:	Arthur Bauer
	Todd McDonald
	Esther Vanier
Managing Editor:	Karen Massetti Miller
Designer:	Gayle O'Brien
Cover Design:	Polly Beaver

Published by American Media Inc.
4900 University Avenue
West Des Moines, IA 50266-6769

Library of Congress Catalog Card Number 96-084772
Seraydarian, Patricia E.
Writing for Business Results

Printed in the United States of America
1997
ISBN 1-884926-48-7

Introduction

Have you ever thought, "I wish I were a better writer"? Or perhaps, "I wish I felt more confident that my writing is effective"? Wherever you fall on the scale of writing skills, this book is designed for you.

If you are just beginning your career and need basic help with your business writing, you will find the principles of good business writing in succinct, clear language. If you are an experienced writer who needs a refresher, you will find your skills reinforced and enhanced with this presentation.

How can you get the most out of this book? Begin by completing the Self-Assessment. This will help you establish your present position. Then work through each of the five chapters. While the entire book can be completed in one to two hours, I recommend that you do one chapter at each sitting. This will help you focus on a single topic. When you have been through the chapters, take the Posttest. You will be surprised at how much you have learned.

You will be so pleased with your results that you will want to measure your progress over a period of time. Completing the Skill Maintenance checklist will do that for you. When you finish Chapter 5, be sure to enter the date on the checklist. Then follow the instructions and measure your growth over a year.

Good luck. You have taken the first step toward improved writing. Turn the page and continue the journey.

About the Author

Patricia E. Seraydarian is the president and principal trainer of C-TIP, Inc., in Las Vegas, Nevada. She has had extensive professional experience as a consultant and trainer in corporate, government, and academic settings. A member of many professional organizations, she is the author of more than a dozen books. Her clients include Michigan Consolidated Gas Company, Livonia Public Schools, and the Business Technology Center of Oakland Community College. Dr. Seraydarian received her Ph.D. from the University of Michigan.

Self-Assessment

How do you feel about your business-writing ability? The simple self-assessment that follows may confirm your confidence or may suggest areas for improvement. In either case, it will provide a starting point for you as you begin *Writing for Business Results.*

		Almost Always	Sometimes	Almost Never
1.	I feel very confident when writing letters and memos.	____	____	____
2.	When writing, getting started is easy for me.	____	____	____
3.	I feel very confident that the format of my letters conforms to standard practices.	____	____	____
4.	I always plan before writing.	____	____	____
5.	I feel sure my opening paragraphs capture the attention of my reader.	____	____	____
6.	I gather all of my information and check any necessary details before writing.	____	____	____
7.	I am careful to state what I want the reader to do.	____	____	____
8.	My letters always close with a clincher.	____	____	____
9.	I limit my letters and memos to one page if possible.	____	____	____
10.	I limit my paragraphs to single ideas.	____	____	____
11.	My electronic messages always get results.	____	____	____

		Almost Always	Sometimes	Almost Never
12.	The five Cs of business writing (conciseness, completeness, courtesy, clarity, correctness) are always identifiable in my writing.	_____	_____	_____
13.	I am confident that the spelling and grammar in my documents are always correct.	_____	_____	_____
14.	I consciously avoid redundant expressions, jargon, clichés, and sexism in my writing.	_____	_____	_____
15.	I wish I could improve my business writing skills.	_____	_____	_____

● Table of Contents

Self-Assessment

Chapter One

Creating Effective Letters 8

Understanding Why You Write Letters 8
Four Critical Questions 9
Planning the Letter 11
Letter Parts 12
The Appearance of Your Letters 17
Projecting a Contemporary Image 18
Format Styles 19
Putting It All Together 21
Chapter Checkpoints 23

Chapter Two

Writing Interoffice Memos 24

Improving Your Memo Image 25
Formatting the Memo 26
Planning the Memo 28
Preparing to Write the Memo 29
Writing the Memo 31
Putting It All Together 34
The Electronic Message—An Instant Memo 36
Chapter Checkpoints 37

Chapter Three

The Five Cs of Good Writing 38

Defining the Five Cs 38
Sample Letters 48
Putting It All Together 50

Chapter Four

The Writer's Edge   52

Principle 1: Use as Few Words as Possible   52
Principle 2: Never Use Two Words When One Will Do   54
Principle 3: Use Positive Words and Phrases   55
Principle 4: Avoid Clichés and Use Jargon Only When
    Appropriate   56
Principle 5: Be Aware of Sexism   57
Principle 6: Use the Active Voice   59
Principle 7: Write *to*, Not *Down to*, Your Reader   60
Principle 8: Big Words Are Unnecessary   61
Principle 9: Write Directly to the Interests of the Reader 63
Principle 10: Are the Details Correct?   64
Putting It All Together   66

Chapter Five

Using the Right Words   68

Frequently Misspelled Words   68
Frequently Confused Words   69
Using Correct Grammar   73
Putting It All Together   78

Posttest   80

Sample Letters   84

Answers to Selected Exercises   89

Skill Maintenance   96

Chapter *One*

Creating Effective Letters

Chapter Objectives

▶ Understand why you write letters.

▶ Plan your writing for success.

▶ Write each part of the letter to achieve the desired result.

▶ Format correspondence to project a contemporary image.

Case Study

Carlos Gonzalez is a very careful writer. He puts considerable time and effort into the many letters he writes during a normal business day. However, he often feels frustrated because his readers either do not respond or they call for additional information. Sometimes he wonders why he works so hard at writing. He suspects that much of his correspondence is not even read.

If this sounds familiar, then Chapter 1 is written just for you.

Understanding Why You Write Letters

We write to get results.

Have you ever asked yourself why you write letters? Perhaps you think that is a foolish question. The truth is, most of us write without ever asking this critical question. Perhaps we don't ask the question because the answer is obvious: *We write to get results.*

The next question is, how often do your letters bring the desired results? Almost always, usually, or less often than you wish? What are the secrets of successful business letters—letters that get results?

Four Critical Questions

You can write letters that bring results if you answer four questions before you begin to write.

Why Am I Writing?

What is your reason for writing? The majority of business letters are written for one of the following purposes:

◆ To convey information.

◆ To invite or respond.

◆ To inquire or request.

◆ To express appreciation or regret.

◆ To remind.

◆ To move to action.

If you cannot identify a specific purpose for writing, perhaps you don't need to write a letter. A phone call or a visit might achieve your goals.

> **If you cannot identify a specific purpose for writing, perhaps you don't need to write a letter.**

To Whom Am I Writing?

What do you know about your reader? When you know the personality of your reader, you have the advantage of tailoring your letter. When you don't know your reader, or when your reader is part of a generic group (i.e., clients or customers), you must write your letters to communicate a warm human element.

What Information or Message Must I Convey?

Have your facts in order before you begin to write. Eliminate unnecessary or nice-to-know information. Focus on the main message.

What Results Do I Want?

What do you want your reader to do? How do you want your reader to respond? If you don't know, your reader won't know either.

Take a Moment

Read the text of the letter below, and answer each of the following questions. Answers appear on page 89.

Dear Ms. Portfena:

The National Association of Women Entrepreneurs is holding its annual meeting January 15–18, 1999, in New Orleans. Because you are one of the most successful entrepreneurs in the United States, we would like to invite you to be the keynote speaker at our closing banquet on January 18 at 6:30 p.m. in the Magnolia Ballroom of the Bayou Plaza Hotel.

My assistant, Gladys Abdul, will call you next week to determine whether you can accept the invitation.

We need to complete our planning within the next 30 days. On behalf of the planning committee, I want to express our eagerness to have you speak at our meeting.

Sincerely,

1. Why was the letter written? Refer to the reasons for writing on page 9. Which one applies to this letter?

    _____

2. How well do you think the writer knows the reader?

    ❑ Very well   ❑ Somewhat acquainted
    ❑ Not personally acquainted   ❑ Not at all

3. Does the letter convey a warm, human element?

    ❑ Yes   ❑ No   ❑ Not Certain

4. What information was necessary? List the facts needed by the reader.

    _____

    _____

5. What results does the writer want? List the results the writer is seeking.

    _____

    _____

Prescription for Writer's Block

The cure for writer's block is to begin writing. Use your letter plan and write a first draft. If time permits, put it aside and revise it later. The most experienced writers will tell you that they write, rewrite, and rewrite again—before writing the final copy.

1

Planning the Letter

Every successful letter begins with a plan. The plan may be a formal outline or, more typically, an informal list of the contents.

Planning your letter involves three steps:

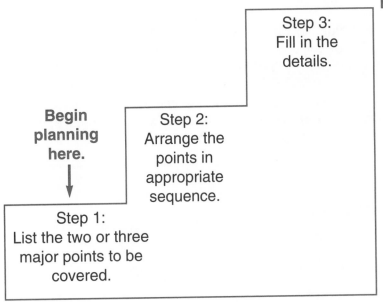

Begin writing here.

Step 3:
Fill in the details.

Begin planning here.

Step 2:
Arrange the points in appropriate sequence.

Step 1:
List the two or three major points to be covered.

Take a Moment

Complete the following exercise. A suggested solution appears on page 89.

Last Friday, you completed a three-session training seminar entitled "Career Planning for the Year 2000" at your local community college. You need to write a letter verifying your attendance for your personnel file. Write your letter plan.

Step 1: List the major points to be covered.

_____

_____

_____

_____

Step 2: Number the items you listed above in the order in which they will appear in the letter by writing 1, 2, 3, or 4 in the space at the left of each line.

Step 3: Since this is only practice, you will skip Step 3—filling in the details—in this exercise. In actual practice, you will always complete this step before you begin to write.

Letter Parts

Most letters contain three to four parts, as appropriate:

◆ An opening or instruction

◆ The main message

◆ A statement of results desired

◆ The closing

The Opening

Four critical seconds—business correspondence specialists tell us that's how long you have to get the attention of your reader.

The *opening* must get the attention of the reader. It contains your topic sentence—your reason for writing. A dull opening suggests a dull letter—one that may not even be read, let alone generate a response.

You have four seconds to get your reader's attention.

Weak Openings	Improved Openings
We have received your letter of June 25, 1999, confirming your plan to speak to our group.	**Thank you for confirming your plans to speak to our group.**
Obvious fact. If you had not received a letter, would you be writing this letter?	Combines a warm thank-you with a brief statement of the purpose of the letter.
This letter is to inform you of the upcoming Executive Committee meeting.	**The Executive Committee will meet on Thursday, July 27, at 2 p.m. in the Spring Mountain Room of the Southwest Hotel.**
Don't talk about it—do it!	Gives the reader all the important facts in the first paragraph.
We have made attempts to collect the past due amount on your account.	**We are frustrated! We have tried unsuccessfully to collect the $159.15 owed us on your account #7Qr54.**
A good beginning, but leaves out the facts.	An unusual opening that is sure to catch the attention of the reader. Leaves no doubt in the reader's mind about the purpose of the letter.

The Main Message

The *main message* contains all the necessary information and details you need to convey. It can be taken directly from a carefully written letter plan.

The *main message* contains all the necessary information and details you need to convey.

Weak Main Messages	Improved Main Messages
Jane Doe was an honors student at Summerin College during the late 1980s and early 1990s.	**Jane Doe attended Summerlin College from September 1988 through June 1992. She graduated magna cum laude from the School of Education.**
Verifies the fact that she was enrolled at the college but gives few additional—and needed—details.	Gives detailed information about Jane's college experience.
Leo Fritelli is a former employee of Magna Corporation. His work was always excellent.	**Leo Fritelli was employed by Magna Corporation as a systems analyst from June 15, 1985, to September 30, 1989. Leo's individual work was always superior, and his teamwork was excellent. We were sorry to lose Leo, but we understood his reasons for seeking another position.**
Verifies his employment without giving any details. Would not be helpful to a potential employer.	Gives detailed information about Leo's employment. Adds a warm, personal note in the final sentence.

The Action or Results

When appropriate, state what information you are seeking or what results you desire. Be specific. Do not leave your reader wondering what you want.

Do not leave your reader wondering what you want.

Weak Request	Improved Requests
Please confirm your appointment as soon as possible.	**Please confirm your appointment by calling my administrative assistant at Extension 2655 no later than Friday, July 15.**
States request vaguely. Does not give the reader the information needed to comply with the request.	States the action desired in definite terms.
The preliminary audit report would be helpful at our meeting next week.	**Plan to bring the preliminary audit report with you when we meet with the comptroller next week.**
Suggests possible action rather than makes a firm request.	States specifically what is needed and when it is needed.

The Closing

The *closing* of
your letter may
take any of
several forms.

The *closing* of your letter may take any of several forms, as determined by the nature of the letter. It may be a summary of the major ideas, a simple statement of goodwill, or a clincher to motivate the reader.

Weak Closings	Improved Closings
Thank you in advance.	**Thank you so much for your patience in this matter.**
A presumptuous closing. Never assume the reader's actions.	Combines an always appropriate thank-you with a specific comment.
You can order this special communications package by calling us today.	**A phone call from you will enable you to enjoy the advantage of online communications immediately.**
The reader knows the product is available. This closing does nothing to clinch the deal.	This closing has the reader is mind. It's to the reader's advantage to place an order—a good clincher.

The Appearance of Your Letters

Case Study 1

■ Marissa Nenadvich is a skilled letter writer. She carefully plans each letter before she writes it. She always reads her letters to be certain she has included all pertinent information. She makes a concentrated effort to stress the reader's point of view and writes with warm tones. Yet, she often fails to get results, particularly when writing to persons she does not know.

She took several samples of her writing to a communications consultant, who promptly identified her problem—the appearance of her letters. She was puzzled because the format of her letters is consistent with the format of letters found in her predecessor's files. Marissa soon learned that her formatting skills were outdated.

Someone once said, "You never get a second chance to make a first impression." That statement is true of your letters.

You never get a second chance to make a first impression.

Writing for results involves not only the contents of the letter but also the appearance of the letter. Some readers may make a decision on whether or not to read and respond to your letter solely on how it looks. Whether you are the originator of the letter or the support staff person who keys and prints the document, you must be aware of how a letter should look if it is to bring results.

Projecting a Contemporary Image

What is appropriate formatting for today's business letter? What recent style changes can you incorporate into your letters to enhance their overall appearance? How can you send a nonverbal message that says you understand that both appearance and content contribute to successful business writing? These suggestions will help you.

◆ Your letters should be consistent with one of the styles illustrated on pages 19 and 20.

◆ The date should appear in the following order: January 1, 1999. The military form 1 January 1999 is appropriate only for military or international correspondence.

◆ The salutations *Dear Sir* and *Gentlemen* are dated. *Dear Sirs* is never used. Use the addressee's name or title, for example, *Dear Mr. Thomas* or *Dear Manager*, whenever possible. When writing to a group, *Ladies and Gentlemen* is the accepted salutation.

Single-space the body of the letter; double-space between paragraphs.

◆ Single-space the body of the letter; double-space between paragraphs. Indent text paragraphs only if you are observing the modified block style. Listings and enumerated items may be indented one tab stop from the left margin.

◆ The name of the writer's company is not included in the closing lines since it appears in the letterhead.

◆ Less formal closings, such as *Sincerely* rather than *Respectfully,* are preferred.

◆ The typist's initials, not the writer's, are included in lowercase in the reference notation. The notation should read abc, not JBK/abc.

◆ Copy notations should reflect the use of photocopies rather than carbon paper, reading *c, copy,* or *PC* rather than *cc.*

Format Styles

Letter formats should be consistent with one of the two styles shown on these pages. Most people are more familiar with the modified block style.

1

Block Style Letter

```
                    BAY VIEW CONSULTANTS
             4750 Landsdowne Place—Suite 555
                    Annapolis, MD 21401
(410) 770-2010                        FAX (410) 770-2015

May 25, 1999

The Norris Agency
330 Riverside Drive
Baltimore, MD 21295

Ladies and Gentlemen

Thank you for your letter of May 23, 1999, confirming our
appointment on June 2, 1999, in your offices. You will be
pleased to learn that Shultua Liang, our executive vice
president who has a strong interest in your agency, plans to
join us.

We will prepare the following items for our meeting:
  • Proposal for the new Norris advertising campaign.
  • Preliminary artwork for the campaign.
  • Detailed information on the timelines for the campaign.

We think you will be very excited when you see this
proposal. It is uniquely Norris and will enhance the
positive image you already enjoy in the advertising world.

Sincerely


M.G. Ashton
Executive Director

lkj
```

◆ All lines begin at the left.

◆ The date begins approximately one inch below the letterhead—this position is adjusted for very short or very long letters.

◆ Open punctuation is used—no colon after the salutation, and no comma after the closing.

◆ A listing begins at the left margin or is indented.

Modified Block Letter

```
              METROPLEX MEDICAL ASSOCIATES, P.C.
                    4500 Professional Plaza
                    Forth Worth, TX 76123
   (817) 363-1950                         FAX (817) 363-1951


                         May 25, 1999

   Massena Pharmaceuticals
   P.O. Box 224
   Massena, NY 13662

   Ladies and Gentlemen:

   Thank you for the prompt shipment of our order No. 30U25-P.
   However, in checking the contents of the order, we found the
   following discrepancies:

        15 doz. Super-X gloves ordered      10 doz. received
        10 doz. No. 15 bandages ordered     15 doz. received

   Invoice No. 45-PQ-3459, enclosed with the order, lists the
   items as we ordered them. Rather than adjust the shipment at
   this point, would you please adjust the invoice to reflect
   the shipment as received and send us a corrected copy.

                         Sincerely,


                         Rose Levine
                         Office Manager

   ytt
```

- ◆ The date and closing lines begin at center.

- ◆ Standard punctuation is used—a colon after the salutation and a comma after the complimentary close.

- ◆ Paragraphs may be blocked or indented.

Putting It All Together

Now that you have reviewed the basic principles of planning
and writing business letters, it is time to put your new skills
to work. Refer to the preceding pages as often as you need to.
First, prepare a letter plan for the situation described below;
then compose the paragraphs of the letter.

■ Situation: Write a letter in response to a customer who
requests information on the newest version of the software
developed by your company. The new version will not be
available until early next year and will include many
enhancements suggested by current users. Pricing
information is not available at this time.

Use the space below to prepare your letter plan.

_____

_____

_____

_____

_____

_____

_____

_____

_____

_____

_____

_____

_____

_____

Reminder: Did you sequence the items? A suggested solution
is on page 89.

You may wish to prepare a first draft of the letter on a separate sheet of paper. This page may be used for the final copy.

You will find a suggested solution on page 90. This solution is only a suggested one. Look at the points the suggested letter makes. Compare them to those in your letter.

Chapter Checkpoints

Writing Checkpoints

◆ Did you begin with a writing plan?

◆ Did you limit each paragraph to one major idea?

◆ When possible, did you limit paragraphs to five or six lines each?

◆ Have you used listings for lengthy details rather than narratives?

◆ Did you remember that one-page letters are always preferable?

◆ Did you check all details before writing the final copy?

Formatting Checkpoints

◆ Scan the letter. Is it placed attractively on the page? Does it appear balanced with your letterhead? Clue: Use the center page feature of your software.

◆ Did you use the default margins of your software (usually one inch)?

◆ Is the format consistent with one of the two accepted styles—block or modified block?

◆ What is the readability quotient of your letter? Does it include:

• Short paragraphs?

• A single, clear typeface?

• A ragged-right margin?

• Lots of white space?

Chapter *Two*

Writing Interoffice Memos

Chapter Objectives

▶ Develop your "memo image."

▶ Write memos with a purpose.

▶ Master the principles of successful memo writing.

▶ Transmit effective electronic messages.

Case Study

Curtis Harrea, office manager at Superior Office Products, writes several memos every day. In fact, since his responsibilities are internal, he seldom writes a letter.

Recently, he distributed a memo that contained some very important information. Later, he overheard two of his employees talking: "Doesn't Curtis have anything else to do but write memos? They are always too long!" The second employee replied, "I've learned to glance at the subject line; if I think it's a 'must read,' I do. Otherwise, it goes in my 'do later' pile. Someone should just tell him that enough is enough!"

Are your memos taken seriously?

This scene is repeated in too many offices every day. Are your memos taken seriously? Chapter 2 will help you take a critical look at your memo-writing practices and provide you with guidelines to increase the acceptability factor of your memos.

Improving Your Memo Image

Do you find that you read and write more memos than letters? If so, you are typical of today's business writer.

Do you feel confident that you can write a memo that commands attention and gets results? Since memos represent internal communication, they tend to accumulate in other people's files, including those of your superiors. What is the memo image of your file?

Is your image fresh? Does a glance at your memos invite reading? Does the content of your memos convey conciseness, preciseness, inclusiveness, and warmth? Or are your memos dull? Are they wordy, indefinite, stilted, and even unnecessary?

2

Today's business writer reads and writes more memos than letters.

Formatting the Memo

Your memo image begins with the appearance of the memo.

Your memo image begins with the appearance of the memo. Apply these checkpoints to the sample memo on the following page.

◆ Is it one page in length?

◆ Are related items aligned?

◆ Are the paragraphs short?

◆ If you scan the memo, does it look readable—and thus invite reading?

◆ When appropriate, have you used a list format rather than a narrative?

◆ Does it contain as much white space as possible?

```
MEMORANDUM

TO:         Yehuda Vitko
FROM:       Gilbert Koslov
DATE:       August 9, 1999
SUBJECT:    RENO BPW MEETING

Thanks so much for agreeing to speak to the Reno
BPW convention on October 15, 1999. The members
of this group are true professionals, and you
will find this opportunity is a delightful
challenge.

The details are:
Reno Business and Professional Women
Admirals Hotel—Marina Room
October 15, 1999
12 noon closing luncheon
20-minute presentation on topic of your choice

Your contact person, Joyce Chung, will call you
within the next few days.

jjk
```

2

Did you notice that you can answer each of these checkpoints simply by scanning the memo, without having to read it? That's what *image* means—a first impression.

Planning the Memo

Interoffice memos may be printed on plain paper or printed forms.

Interoffice memos may be printed on plain paper or printed forms. In either case, four items always appear:

- The name of the addressee(s).

- The name of the originator.

- The date the memo is written.

- The subject of the memo.

Printed forms may have additional fill-in lines.

Checkpoints for Memo Details

- When a memo is being sent to several people, replace individual names with a distribution list. List names of recipients below the last line of the message.

- As a rule, place the names in the distribution list in alphabetical order. Or you may place names in order of seniority or rank within the organization. Caution: A ranked list leaves open the possibility of misplacing a name.

  - Do not use job titles in memos.

  - Use a descriptive subject line.

  - Replace the signature line by the handwritten initials of the originator at the top of the memo.

Preparing to Write the Memo

Writing is easy when you remember that determining your purpose for writing *precedes* preparing a writing plan, which *precedes* writing a first draft, which *precedes* writing a final copy.

Effective writing always begins with planning. Planning begins when you answer one critical question.

What do I want the reader to know or do after reading this memo?

Once you have determined what you want the reader to know or do, you are ready to plan the memo. Planning is a three-step process, as illustrated in the following diagram:

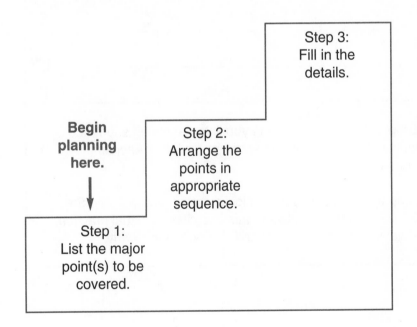

Begin writing here.

Step 3:
Fill in the details.

Begin planning here.
↓

Step 2:
Arrange the points in appropriate sequence.

Step 1:
List the major point(s) to be covered.

2

Take a Moment

Complete the following exercise. A suggested solution appears on page 90.

■ Kay Sanchez, mail supervisor for Southwest Products, must write a memo to initiate the following three changes in mailing procedures: Mail to be sent by a private carrier must be received by 3:30 p.m. Overnight mail must be received by 4:00 p.m. Mail must be received in the mail room by 4:30 p.m. to be mailed the same day. These changes are to take effect July 15.

Step 1: List the major points to be covered. (Four lines are provided; you may have fewer or more points.)

_____

_____

_____

_____

Step 2: Number the points you listed above in sequence by writing 1, 2, 3, or 4 in the space at the left of each line above.

Step 3: Since this is a practice exercise, you will skip Step 3—filling in the details—in this exercise. In actual practice, always complete this step before you begin to write.

Writing the Memo

The Opening

The most important information in your memo, including conclusions or recommendations, belongs in the first sentence or paragraph.

Writing in this way captures your reader's attention immediately and makes your reason for writing clear. It sets the stage for action or decisions.

Read the following opening paragraph:

■ Sometimes big corporations are accused of being indifferent to human needs. I think that is why I was so pleased to learn of a recent series of events that involved a group of our employees in the Dayton plant.

What important information is conveyed in this paragraph? Does it really grab your interest? Or do you respond in a "Ho-hum, that's nice" manner? How would you respond to the paragraph below if you received this memo in the middle of a hectic day in which everything had gone wrong?

■ Verma White, a maintenance technician in our Dayton plant who found herself and her six children homeless just six months ago, is a proud new homeowner—thanks to the efforts of 23 of her coworkers.

Would you agree that this opening paragraph is more intriguing, leading you to continue reading? The main point is in the first paragraph.

2

**Memo Secret 1:
Put the message
up front.**

The Main Message

The succeeding paragraphs of your memo briefly support the important information already conveyed in the first paragraph. Only pertinent information is included. Nice-to-know information does not have a place in memos.

Listing may be used very effectively with some types of information. Compare the following main message paragraphs of a memo.

■ You might wish to consider the following topics as you plan your presentation: Quality Circles, Management with Meaning, The Corporate Ladder Has a Missing Rung, You Ain't There Yet!, or High-Tech with High-Touch. Since our members are true professionals, I think any of these would be well received.

■ Possible topics include:
- Quality Circles
- Management with Meaning
- The Corporate Ladder Has a Missing Rung
- You Ain't There Yet!
- High-Tech with High-Touch

Notice how much more readable the second sample is? Even a quick read conveys the message.

The Closing

Unlike business letters, the best memo closing may be none. Use a closing only when you need to convey a last item of information.

Compare the following closing paragraphs of a memo.

■ When you have had an opportunity to consider all the options, please give me a call. If you have any questions, please do not hesitate to contact me.

**Memo Secret 3:
Eliminate
unnecessary
closings.**

This closing contains no necessary information. And it is weakened by the vague reference, "please give me a call." It continues its ineffectiveness by closing with a cliché: "If you have any questions, please do not hesitate to contact me."

Can this closing by improved? No. It is unnecessary and therefore should not even be written.

■ Please meet in my office on Tuesday, August 3, at 9:00 a.m. to finalize these plans.

This is an example of a closing paragraph that is effective—written in brief, specific language.

Putting It All Together

Now that you have reviewed the basic principles of planning and writing memos, it is time to put your new skills to work. Refer to the preceding pages as often as necessary.

First, prepare a memo plan for the situation described below. Then, write a first draft of the memo. Finally, do any necessary rewriting or editing for a final copy.

■ Write a memo to all department managers telling them that the preliminary architectural plans for a building expansion are ready to be reviewed. These plans will be presented by Letitia Villacorta, president of your company, at a meeting on Tuesday of next week in your office. Each manager should bring 12 copies of the respective five-year department plans. This is an exciting meeting because these plans have been in the works for 36 months.

Use the space here and on the next page to prepare your memo-writing plan.

_____

_____

_____

_____

_____

_____

_____

_____

_____

_____

_____

_____

_____

_____

Reminder: Did you sequence the points? A suggested solution is on page 90.

You may wish to prepare the first draft on a separate sheet of paper. Use the space below to draft your final memo.

_____

_____

_____

_____

_____

_____

_____

_____

_____

_____

_____

_____

_____

_____

_____

_____

_____

_____

_____

_____

A suggested solution appears on page 90. Look at the important points in the suggested memo. Compare them to those in your memo.

The Electronic Message— An Instant Memo

The use of electronic messages is growing rapidly. It has been established that by the year 2000, 60 billion messages will be sent annually. What do you need to know to use this medium successfully?

Electronic messages are another form of interoffice memos. Many of the checkpoints from this chapter also apply to electronic messages. In addition, the following guidelines will be helpful to you.

Electronic Message Secret: Remember, there is a human being at the other end of the line.

Effective Electronic Messages

◆ The reader cannot see your face; thus, the nuances of communication are missing. Avoid jokes, sarcasm, threats, or any tools of verbal communication that might be misinterpreted.

◆ Write an attention-getting opening sentence. As more and more messages are sent, yours must stand out if it is to be read.

◆ Write the main message—and the main message only.

◆ Limit your message to one screen, if possible.

◆ Review your message before sending it. Is it grammatically correct? Are all words spelled correctly? Your image and your credibility are on the line.

◆ Avoid using the system for personal messages. Electronic messages may not be as private as you think.

◆ Be sure you save or print a copy when you need a record of your message.

Chapter Checkpoints

Memo-Writing Checkpoints

◆ Always begin with a writing plan.

◆ Put the most important information in the first sentence of the paragraph.

◆ Tell the reader what you want done as quickly as possible.

◆ Write short, simple sentences.

◆ When appropriate, use a listing to expand or support the main message.

◆ Eliminate all unnecessary information.

◆ Eliminate unnecessary closings.

Memo Protocol

◆ Never write a memo you are unwilling to have other people read.

◆ Never assume that memo information will be kept confidential.

◆ Never ignore the chain of command.

◆ Avoid exaggeration.

◆ Avoid humor; never use sarcasm.

◆ Don't use a memo to criticize another person or department.

◆ If you write a negative memo, delay sending it.

Chapter *Three*
The Five Cs of Good Writing

Chapter Objectives

▶ Understand the application of the five Cs of good writing business-writing success.

▶ Master the application of the five Cs on business copy.

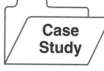

Case Study

Brigitte Svensen, medical office supervisor, composes many explanatory letters to patients, referral doctors, and hospitals and extended care administrators. The nature of her correspondence has taught her to be careful with details. But she still lacks confidence in her overall writing ability. She wonders whether there is a simple set of guidelines that she could use to evaluate her own writing.

Brigitte would find Chapter 3 very helpful. The Five Cs are universal guidelines to good writing. Observing the Five Cs will help you write more effective letters and memos.

Defining the Five Cs

What are the five Cs that are so important to good writing?

1. **Conciseness**
   Write the message in as few words as possible.

2. **Completeness**
   Ensure that all information needed by the reader to respond or act is included.

3. **Courtesy**
   Show consideration for the reader.

4. **Clarity**
   Write clearly.

5. **Correctness**
   Check the letter or memo for accuracy of all statements and details.

Conciseness

Conciseness means writing the message in as few words as possible. Being concise does not always mean being brief. For example, you may write a 20-page report that is concise if it says only what is necessary.

Being concise means avoiding unnecessary explanations. If the added information is not important to the main message, don't include it.

Being concise means avoiding three common writing traps: excess words, redundancies, and long words in place of short ones. Study the examples below of each of these.

Conciseness means writing the message in as few words as possible.

3

Wordiness

First draft: As much as I would like to meet you for lunch on Thursday, I cannot because my 7-year-old granddaughter, Rochelle, is having her first tap-dance recital on that date. I have an 11:00 appointment on Monday, but I think I will be finished in time for lunch. Is your schedule free on that date?

Revision: I am unable to join you for lunch on Thursday. Could we reschedule for Monday?

Redundancies

First draft: Past experience tells me that our first priority should be consideration of the final outcome.

Revision: Experience suggests that our priority should be consideration of the outcome.

Long Words

First draft: We need to maximize our profits in the coming quarter.

Revision: We need to add to our profits in the next quarter.

Completeness

> *Completeness means ensuring that all information needed by the reader to respond or act is included.*

Completeness means ensuring that all information needed by the reader to respond or act is included. Completeness involves presenting all the facts.

◆ If you ask a person to call, include a phone number.

◆ If you invite a person to a meeting, give the date, the time, and the place.

◆ If you expect the reader to take action, present all the facts necessary to do so.

◆ If you are making a recommendation, provide supporting data.

Study the following examples for a better understanding of completeness.

Missing Details

First draft: Please call me when you reach your decision.

Revision: Please call me at 702-225-1990 when you reach your decision.

First draft: Please meet me on Tuesday at 2:00 p.m.

Revision: Please meet me on Tuesday, September 15, at 2:00 p.m. in the Executive Conference Room at Metro Airport.

3

Missing Facts or Data

First draft: My department members simply cannot tolerate the continued tardiness of Janet Adams. My recommendation is immediate termination.

Revision: The continued tardiness of Ms. Adams (see below) is having a negative effect on my department members, and I recommend immediate termination.

Janet Adams	Emp. No. 363-89-7878
Verbal Warning	Feb. 1, 1993
Late 5 min.	Feb. 15, 1993
Late 7 min.	Feb. 22, 1993
Late 15 min.	Feb. 23, 1993
First written warning	Feb. 28, 1993
Late 10 min.	Mar. 2, 1993
Late 15 min.	Mar. 5, 1993

Courtesy

Courtesy involves showing consideration for the reader. Courtesy is self-explanatory. It refers to using words such as *please* and *thank you* as often as appropriate. Courtesy also involves keeping the reader's interests and feelings in mind. The courteous letter uses positive words and phrases rather than negative ones.

Even "bad news" letters can be courteous and warm. When you are faced with a bad news/good news situation, always deliver the bad news first. Then write the good news, adding emphasis to it by putting it at the end of the sentence.

Lack of Courtesy

First draft: Your response to our letter last week arrived today.

Revision: Thank you for responding so quickly to our letter.

Negative Expressions

First draft: You claimed in your complaint letter . . .

Revision: You stated in your letter . . .

Bad News/Good News

First draft: I would recommend that you contact Manuel Martinez since I çannot accept your invitation to speak to your group.

Revision: Since I am unable to accept your invitation to speak to your group, I would like to suggest that you call Manuel Martinez, who is an excellent speaker.

Clarity

Clarity simply means writing clearly. Clarity involves being specific. A clear letter or memo leaves no doubts in the reader's mind.

Promote clarity in your writing. Jargon exists in every industry, is understood by insiders, and may be appropriate for in-house communications. However, jargon is unfamiliar to outsiders, and is not appropriate for outside correspondence.

You may find that you can improve the clarity of your writing by controlling the length of your sentences. Generally, aim for 10 to 14 words per sentence.

Clarity simply means writing clearly.

3

Vague Expression

First draft: The change in managers will have a major impact on our sales forecasts. (Will the impact be positive or negative?)

Revision: The change in managers will have a major negative impact on our sales forecasts.

Vague Noun

First draft: The woman bought a new black puppy.

Revision: Mayor Susan Marx bought a black Doberman puppy.

Jargon

First draft: We need to interface about the bug in the CPU.

Revision: We need to talk about the problem with your computer.

Long Sentence

First draft: Hopefully, I will be able to expedite the termination notice to achieve processing no later than the fifteenth of January.

Revision: I hope to wrap up the termination process by January 15.

Correctness

Correctness involves checking the letter or memo for accuracy of all statements and details. Remember Smokey Bear's slogan, "Only you can prevent forest fires!"? Only you, the writer, can check for accuracy of statements and details. Another person reading your work may be totally uninformed.

Be particularly careful to proofread numbers, such as dates, times, amounts of money, and so forth.

Make sure the statement says what you intend it to say. Check the usage of similar words, such as affect/effect and less/fewer. Refer to Chapter 5 for a review of frequently confused words.

Use the spell-checking feature of your word processor. But remember, a spell checker is not a substitute for a careful reading by the writer.

> *Correctness* involves checking the letter or memo for accuracy of all statements and details.

3

Inaccuracy of Statement

First draft: Every one at the meeting agreed we must proceed with the project. (Did everyone agree, or is a consensus more accurate? Only you know.)

Revision: The consensus of those present was that we must proceed with the project.

Inaccuracy of Numbers

First draft: We will be closed on Thanksgiving Day, November 25, 1992. (In 1992, Thanksgiving falls on November 26.)

Revision: We will be closed on Thanksgiving Day, November 26, 1992.

Misuse of Similar Words

First draft: Its only three miles further down the road.

Revision: It's only three miles farther down the road.

Errors Overlooked by Spell Checker

First draft: Margeaux and Petros were to tired to finish there report.

Revision: Margeaux and Petros were too tired to finish their report.

Take a Moment

You have just learned five basic principles of business writing. You now have an opportunity to apply this knowledge by improving each of the following sentences. On the lines provided, rewrite each sentence. Suggested solutions appear on page 91.

Conciseness:
It has come to my attention that our employees, new and old, have developed a habit of taking extended coffee and lunch breaks.

_____

_____

Completeness:
Your performance review will be next Tuesday morning.

_____

_____

Courtesy:
Your failure to send in your monthly payment upsets me.

_____

_____

Clarity:
A comprehensive review of your in-house substance-abuse program will be conducted by members of the local university's Wellness Division.

_____

_____

Correctness:
Four months have only 30 days: April, June, September, and October.

_____

_____

Sample Letters
First draft

Note lack of:

Conciseness/
Clarity

Completeness

Correctness

Courtesy

GO-RITE LANDSCAPING

P.O. Box 375   Las Vegas, NV 89117

June 23, 1999

Star Nurseries
3500 Cheyenne Ave.
Henderson, NV 89015

Ladies/Gentlemen

It has come to my attention that the fiscus
auricular you have supplied to us in recent weeks
have been very inferior to those you normally
supply. In fact, the last three or four shipments
have been noticeably poor.

Everyone knows that these plants grow well in our
area, and problems simply do not occur.

I expect you to take care of this matter
immediately.

Sincerely

Gary Rodeghier
President

pr

Revision

GO-RITE LANDSCAPING

P.O. Box 375   Las Vegas, NV 89117

June 23, 1999

Star Nurseries
3500 Cheyenne Ave.
Henderson, NV 89015

Ladies/Gentlemen

Our orders of June 2, 15, and 20 each included
eight fiscus trees (5'). The trees shipped to us
were not of your usual high quality. We anticipated
needing to replace some of these for our customers.

Since fiscus trees normally do well in our area,
our initial assumption is that the problem lies
with the grower. Would you please look into this
matter and call me at 702-225-1900 as soon as you
have some information?

Sincerely

Gary Rodeghier
President

pr

3

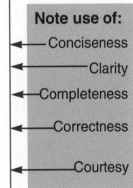

Note use of:
Conciseness
Clarity
Completeness
Correctness
Courtesy

Putting It All Together

You are now ready to put it all together and apply the five Cs of business writing to a sample letter.

Look at the text of the letter below. A quick reading will convince you that the writer either is unaware of the principles of writing or chooses to ignore them. You may find it helpful to review the five Cs. You may wish to highlight specific instances where one of the principles should have been applied.

February 1, 1999

Martin G. LeFavre
3301 Eastern Ave., Apt. 211
Wichita, KS 67215

Dear Marty

Your letter of application for an entry-level sales position in our company has been added to our file of active applicants. We do not have any openings at this time.

The file remains open for a period of six months. If you with to be considered after that time, you must submit a new application. Sometimes when we have a particular interest in a person of your qualifications, we will move your application into the new active file. It also helps if you submit to a particular person rather than to the human resources department.

Good luck in your job search!

Sincerely

First, rewrite the letter in the space provided. After you have
written your letter, review it carefully for conciseness,
completeness, courtesy, clarity, and correctness. Can you
identify specific examples of each of the five Cs? A suggested
solution appears on page 91.

3

_____

_____

_____

_____

_____

_____

_____

_____

_____

_____

_____

_____

_____

_____

_____

_____

_____

_____

_____

_____

_____

Chapter *Four*

The Writer's Edge

Case Study

Margareta Gurrieri, a paralegal, took time one day to read some letters she had written. To her dismay, she found that she had fallen into some poor writing habits: She wrote wordy sentences, used jargon frequently, and talked down to the clients. She recognized sentences that would have been more emphatic with the simple use of an active verb. She knew that she needed to brush up on her writing skills.

Chapter 4 is designed to help experienced writers like Margareta, as well as novice writers, improve their writing by using these 10 Write-for-Results Principles.

Principle 1: Use as Few Words as Possible

A recent college graduate began her résumé with the following career objective:

■ Objective:
To be in a position to utilize my excellent educational preparation, my meaningful work experience, and my outstanding people skills in a middle-management position that will give me a good opportunity to grow professionally and personally in very important ways.

Does this statement impress you? Probably not. Would you think, "Just tell me what your objective is!"? The fewer words you use, the more powerful your message is.

Excessive words can easily creep into your writing. Check the list on the left below. Do any of these appear in your writing?

> **Excessive words can easily creep into your writing.**

Excessive Wording	Improved Wording
at a later date	later
at all times	always
at this point in time	now
can be in a position to	can
due to the fact that	because
each and every one	every one
firstly, secondly, thirdly,	first, second, third
in compliance with your request	at your request
in the event of	if
in the majority of instances	usually
inasmuch as	since
on a monthly basis	monthly
owing to the fact that	since

4

Take a Moment

Can you think of wordy expressions you use? List them in the left-handed column below. Can you think of any ways to improve those expressions? Write them in the right-hand column.

_____   _____

_____   _____

_____   _____

_____   _____

_____   _____

Principle 2: Never Use Two Words When One Will Do

Most of us say more than is necessary to make our point. We carry over this habit into writing. The use of redundant expressions is another form of excessive wording. Some redundant expressions have become clichés. For that reason, you may not even recognize them as being redundant.

Can you identify the redundancies in the following sentence?

■ The consensus of opinion is that our advance planning was absolutely essential.

Did you spot *consensus* of opinion, *advance* planning, *absolutely* essential? Look over the following list of other common redundant expressions. Note that each of the italicized words is unnecessary.

actual experience	*final* conclusion
and *etc.*	*first and* foremost
ask *the question*	*following* after
attached *hereto*	for *a period of* two weeks
at some later *date*	*foreign* imports
basic fundamentals	*free* gratis
blend/join/merge/mix *together*	goals *and objectives*
circle *around*	*group* meeting
close proximity/scrutiny	large/small *in size*
collect/combine *together*	*mutual* cooperation
completely filled	*new* innovation
consequent results	*one and* the same
continue *on*	*past* experience
cooperate *together*	plan *ahead/for the future/in advance*
disappear from sight	
enclosed *herewith*	reason *is because*
estimated *to be about*	recur/repeat *again*
exact opposites	same *identical*
few *in numbers*	*true* facts

Underline any of the above expressions that you use. This will increase your awareness of the phrases and help you eliminate them from your writing.

Principle 3: Use Positive Words and Phrases

Do you remember the popular song of the 1940s "Accentuate the Positive!"? Perhaps the composer was also a writer of business letters, because the advice is excellent. Compare the two sentences below.

Negative Statement

You overlooked the fact that you failed to make last month's payment.

Positive Statement

Were you aware that you did not mail last month's payment?

Which statement is more likely to elicit a positive response from the customer? Which one would you respond to?

Negative expressions can be either direct or implied. If a sentence reads, "You are not qualified for the position," it is a direct negative. If the same sentence reads, "You need more experience to qualify for this position," it is negative by implication. Your task as a writer is to convey negative information in positive language.

Remember, your ultimate goal is to bring about a positive response or action from the reader. You accomplish this more quickly if you do not scold or make the reader feel guilty.

Two pointers may help you create positive statements for negative situations:

♦ Avoid beginning a sentence with *you*. A softer sentence results when the *you* is placed within the sentence. "Did you understand my point?" is much softer than "You failed to understand my point."

♦ Substitute *when* for *if.* "When you complete your work, we will process your salary increase" implies confidence in the reader more than "If you complete your work, we will process your salary increase."

> **Remember, your ultimate goal is to bring about a positive response or action from the reader.**

Principle 4: Avoid Clichés and Use Jargon Only When Appropriate

Clichés **are fad phrases and trite expressions.**

Clichés are fad phrases and trite expressions. Americans are experts at creating fad phrases. Initially, these can be very effective. But with overuse, they quickly lose their punch. An example is *user-friendly*, a term that came to us in the early 1980s with PCs. It has long since lost its impact.

There are thousands of clichés in our language. A few of the familiar ones used in business usage are listed here. Be aware of clichés in your own writing and eliminate them.

ballpark figure	enclosed herewith	meaningful
bottom line	first and foremost	prioritize
brainstorm	hands-on	state of the art
cost-effective	input	thank you in advance
dialogue	maximize	

Jargon **is insider talk—words and phrases understood by persons in a particular profession or industry.**

Jargon is insider talk—words and phrases understood by persons in a particular profession or industry. Jargon is a necessary part of communication between persons in the profession, but it is inappropriate when writing to persons outside your industry who may be unfamiliar with it. As we said in Chapter 3, jargon interferes with clarity. Samples of jargon taken from several professions include:

cash cow	extended family	needs assessment
CPU	facilitator interface	normative sample
debug	feasibility study	quality circles
DTP	K	

As you identify jargon in your communications, be sure you observe the following guidelines:

♦ Limit the use of jargon to those readers who understand it.

♦ If you must use jargon, include its meaning the first time you use it.

Principle 5: Be Aware of Sexism

Good business writers are careful to eliminate all sexist language or inferences from their writing. In the past, sexism has been evident in two forms:

◆ The use of sexist designations: mailman or stewardess.

◆ The use of sexist pronoun references: the doctor and his patients, or the nurse and her patients.

Sexism in writing can be eliminated in three ways:

◆ Using *his/her* in place of the single *his* or *her:* Each employee must prepare his/her own report. **Note:** Many writers consider this an awkward construction and avoid it whenever possible.

◆ Changing the noun to a plural form and using *their:* All employees must prepare their own reports.

◆ Rewriting the sentence to avoid the use of a pronoun: Reports must be prepared by individual employees.

Eliminating sexism from your writing does not mean that you accept a certain political system or philosophy. It simply means that you acknowledge the equality of roles that exist in business today. Listed below are samples of gender-specific terms that have changed in recent years.

Original Phrase	Improved Phrase
chairman	chair, chairperson
fireman	firefighter
housewife	homemaker
man hours	work hours
my girl	my secretary/assistant/support person
policeman	police officer
salesman	salesperson
stewardess	flight attendant
workman	worker/employee

4

Take a Moment

Apply the five write-for-results principles you have just reviewed to these sample sentences. Rewrite the following sentences. Suggested solutions are on page 92.

Use as few words as possible:
Pursuant to your personal letter of May 15, 1999, we wish to inform you that the aggregate amount of your purchase leaves an account balance of $259.95.

_____

_____

Eliminate redundant expressions:
It is my personal opinion that the statement attached hereto contains the true facts in the case.

_____

_____

Use positive words and phrases:
If you will take time to read the enclosed brochure, you will understand why we demand prompt payment of all accounts.

_____

_____

Eliminate clichés and jargon:
Thank you in advance for helping us prioritize our needs.

_____

_____

Avoid sexist references:
The future of each employee lies in his own hands.

_____

_____

Principle 6: Use the Active Voice

Perhaps you remember the classic definition: "Active verbs act; passive verbs are acted upon."

Active verb: Our Roanoke branch tests all new products.

Passive Verb: All new products are tested at our Roanoke branch.

Using active verbs adds power to your writing. Active verbs are more dynamic than passive verbs. Active verbs move your reader to action. Active verbs result in shorter sentences.

> **Using active verbs adds power to your writing.**

Passive verbs can be identified by the presence of a linking verb *(is, are, am, was,* or *were).* Compare the two forms below.

4

Active Verb	Passive Verb
communicated	are communicated
analyzed	were analyzed
thought	was thought

Passive verbs in sentences can usually be converted to active verbs by rewriting the sentence. When you rewrite, be careful that you do not change the meaning.

Passive: The new policy was recommended by Gerard.
Active: Gerard recommended the new policy.

Passive: It has been decided to cancel the program.
Active: The Executive Committee canceled the program.

Use the passive voice when the subject of the sentence or the doer of the action is more important than the action, as in the following examples.

■ Minimum standards will be established for all new employees.
(The standards are more important than the employees.)

■ The worker was seriously injured by the falling beam.
(The worker is more important than the beam.)

Principle 7: Write *to*, Not *Down to*, Your Reader

The use of condescending words and phrases in your writing is a more abstract concept than some of the writing principles discussed previously. Condescending expressions are a matter of tone rather than specific words. The same words can be acceptable in one situation and unacceptable (condescending) in another. Condescension is talking down to the reader. The reader senses a scolding or an "I told you so" attitude.

A condescending tone is most apt to creep into your writing when you are displeased with the reader, the reader's action, or lack of the reader's action.

Condescending: As you are well aware, our policy is to satisfy our customers.

Improved: As a valued customer, your satisfaction is our goal.

Notice that the first sentence is me-oriented, and thus condescending. The second sentence is you-oriented. Which one evokes a positive response from you?

Unfortunately, some writers use a condescending tone to boost their own egos or to express their own sense of self-importance. A common way of doing this is through the use of jargon (see Principle 4).

Condescending: The documentation for your LAN will answer all your questions. If you don't understand the instructions, call our technical support system.

Improved: You will find the manual for your network very helpful. If you have additional questions, our support staff at 1-800-225-8989 is eager to help you.

If you had recently installed a computer network, which sentence would you find user-friendly?

Note: Every business writer has moments of anger or exasperation. If you can, avoid writing during those times. If you must write, put the letter or memo aside. Read it later, and alter the tone before sending it.

Principle 8: Big Words Are Unnecessary

Do you want to write power-packed messages? Use short, plain words. Too often, the only person you impress with big words is yourself. Have you ever heard a reader complain that a letter or memo was too easy to understand?

> Too often, the only person you impress with big words is yourself.

Your writing should be appropriate for your audience. Think of the people you most often write to: customers, clients, and colleagues. All these people would rather do business with a warm, helpful human being than a cold, robotlike individual.

4

What about your superiors? Many executives will tell you that they respond to clear, plain, short messages. They do not have time to interpret your impressive use of the language.

Stilted language:	The cessation of the policy will occur at 12:01 a.m., July 15.
Improved language:	The policy expires at 12:01 a.m., July 15.
Too many big words:	You should proceed to investigate the findings of the study.
Improved language:	Continue your study of the findings.

How you can develop the good writing habit of simple language:

◆ Write the message naturally, including any big words that come to you.

◆ Reread the message. Did you write to impress rather than to express?

◆ Ask yourself: What am I really trying to say?

◆ Write down any big words you use unnecessarily. Remember, awareness is the first step to improvement.

Take a Moment

The three writing principles you have just reviewed focused on enhancing your writing skill. Let's apply this skill to sample sentences. Rewrite the following sentences. Suggested solutions are on page 92.

Use active verbs:
The new vacation policy was approved by the employee task force and will give employees of five years or more an added week of vacation.

_____

_____

Avoid a condescending tone:
Since we have done business for many years, you should know that we require payment upon delivery, unless prior arrangements have been made.

_____

_____

Use simple words:
Enclosed herewith is a copy of the recently passed legislative act empowering Kansas City homeowners to appeal the tax rates established for their properties.

_____

_____

Principle 9: Write Directly to the Interests of the Reader

Not considering the interests of your reader could be the reason behind the other nine writing traps. If you consciously consider the interests of your reader, you are apt to observe good writing principles. How can you do this?

Visualize your reader. Imagine that you and your reader are holding a conversation. What level of language would you use? What tone would you convey to maintain a positive discussion? What information would you give that person? What response would you expect? All of these questions represent issues you want to keep in mind when writing. They guarantee that you think of your reader first.

Imagine that you and your reader are holding a conversation.

4

Business-writing books have called this approach the *you attitude*. It emphasizes *you* instead of *I/we/me/us*. Consider the following sentences:

I/Me Attitude	You Attitude
If we do not receive your check immediately, we will be unable to continue shipping your orders without prepayment.	You have always enjoyed immediate shipping status. You can retain this convenient rating by sending us your check immediately.
While I remember with pleasure my appearance last year at your awards banquet, I am not available on July 30 this year to speak to your group.	What a pleasure it was to speak to your group last year. I sincerely wish I could join you again this year but, unfortunately, I have another engagement.

When you are the reader, what letter tone elicits a favorable response? Whenever you write a letter, ask yourself how you would respond if you were the reader.

Principle 10: Are the Details Correct?

■ A local dentist's office routinely sends letters to new patients. The letters are concise, warm, and personal. The message is lost due to poor formatting, typos, and two typefaces. They are obviously form letters, mass-produced on a poor copier.

When the letter is brought to the attention of Jodie Menendez, the dental office manager, she says that it is out of her control because the letter is prepared by a service.

Jodie is responsible. If she has hired a secretarial service, she has a right to expect quality work. The image of the secretarial service is not affected, but the image of the dental practice is tarnished.

Do you think your job is done when you finish writing a letter? Composing the letter is only the first step.

As the writer, you are also responsible for error-free copy, accurate information or details, and appropriate formatting. If you send your letters to a support person for typing, you hope that person will also assume some responsibility for the accuracy of the contents. However, when you sign the letter, you are implying approval of the contents and the appearance. Do you take pride in the letters bearing your signature? Are you reasonably certain of their accuracy?

The quality of your correspondence is a reflection of you. What image are you projecting?

◆ Scan your correspondence before signing it. Does it appear balanced on the page? Is there enough white space to encourage reading?

◆ Read the letter for content. Does it say what you intend to say? Is the tone positive?

◆ Read the letter for accuracy. Are the spelling and grammar correct? Are names, dates, and other details correct?

Take a Moment

You have just completed the review of the final two write-for-results principles: considering the interests of the reader and paying attention to details. Both of these represent important refinements in your writing.

Read the sentences below. Write an improved sentence for each one. Suggested solutions are on page 93.

Consider the interests of the reader:
We are unable to fill your order for one file cabinet because you failed to specify the color and size.

_____

_____

Pay attention to details:
Each of the divisions have made a firm commitment to better quality control.

_____

_____

4

Putting It All Together

Now you are aware of the 10 write-for-results principles of business writing, you are ready to apply them in your writing.

Read the letter below. Remembering the 10 write-for-results principles, can you spot them in this letter? Highlight them for review. Refer to the previous pages as needed.

```
February 20, 1999

Ara Godosian, Manager
ABC Suppliers Inc.
P.O. Box 4857
Neward, NJ 07152

Dear Mr. Godosian

Due to the fact that, in the majority of recent
instances, your account with us has had an overdue
past balance, we can no longer sell merchandise to
you on a cash basis.

We are sorry to take this unfortunate action, but
you have been warned on previous occasions that it
might be necessary.

I must ask the question: What is the problem? Is
your manager of accounts payable unable to keep his
accounts in order? We are sorry, but we have to pay
our bills too. The bottom line is continuing to
carry your account is no longer cost-effective for
us.

Lastly, since my personal experience is working with
you has always been positive, I have asked that your
account be held in our active files for a period of
10 days. If you wish to respond to this action, you
will need to do so within that time frame.

Sincerely


Patrick Monaghan
Controller
```

Rewrite the letter in the space provided here. As you're writing, think about the writing principles. Are there particular ones that you have never applied in your writing? After you've rewritten the letter, review it closely. Have you applied each of the 10 writing principles? A suggested solution appears on page 93.

_____

_____

_____

_____

_____

_____

_____

_____

_____

_____

_____

_____

_____

_____

_____

_____

_____

_____

_____

_____

4

Chapter *Five*

Using the Right Words

> ## Chapter Objectives
>
> ▶ Recognize the most frequently misspelled words in business writing.
>
> ▶ Use correct grammar, recognizing five areas where errors are most likely to occur.

S pelling and grammatical errors can ruin even the best piece of writing. You can avoid these problems by learning to recognize frequently misspelled words and areas where grammatical errors are likely to occur.

Frequently Misspelled Words

The key to improving your spelling is to identify the words you tend to misspell. This is not as difficult as you might think. Many of the spelling errors that appear in business writing occur with the same words. Knowing that these words are potential problems can help you eliminate spelling errors from your writing. Listed here are 25 of the most frequently misspelled words. Do you recognize any words that cause you problems? Circle those words.

> **The key to improving your spelling is to identify the words you tend to misspell. This is not as difficult as you might think.**

accommodate	develop	recommend
achievement	embarrass	separate
acknowledgment	extension	similar
analysis	judgment	supersede
benefited	loose	surprise
calendar	occurrence	
commitment	possession	
convenient	precede	
criticism	privilege	
description	proceed	

After you identify a frequently misspelled word, try to isolate the portion of the word that gives you trouble. The spelling problems in the frequently misspelled words we just identified tend to be the same for most people. Look at the list below. The trouble spot in each word is underlined. Note the trouble spot in the words that you circled.

accommodate	description	privilege
achievement	develop	proceed
acknowledgment	embarrass	recommend
analysis	extension	separate
benefited	judgment	similar
calendar	loose	supersede
commitment	occurrence	surprise
convenient	possession	
criticism	precede	

Frequently Confused Words

Many similar words in our language cause even the most careful writer to pause. For example, when do you use *accept* or *except,* or *to, too,* or *two?* Being able to distinguish between similar words ensures the accuracy of your writing.

Since the spell checker on your word processor will not highlight these words, it is very important for you to know how each one is used.

Review the following list of frequently confused words. Think about each word, its definition, and its use in a sentence.

Being able to distinguish between similar words ensures the accuracy of your writing.

5

Accept, Except:
Accept means to receive something; *except* means to exclude.

■ I cannot accept your explanation.

■ Everyone except the patient was pleased.

Affect, Effect:
Affect means to influence; *effect* (as a noun) means a result; *effect* (as a verb) means to bring about.

■ Will the change affect your plans?

■ The effects were immediately noticeable.

■ How can we effect this change in policy?

All Ready, Already:
All ready means completely prepared; *already* means previously.

■ Is your presentation all ready?

■ It's already lunchtime.

All Right, Alright:
All right means satisfaction; *alright* is nonstandard English and should be avoided.

■ The schedule is all right with me.

Beside, Besides:
Beside means next to; *besides* means in addition to.

■ The printer is beside the desk.

■ Besides Mr. Klein, who is not coming?

Capital, Capitol:
Capital refers to money or the seat of state government; *capitol* refers to the building in which a legislative body meets.

■ How much capital will you need?

■ The capital of Iowa is Des Moines.

■ The citizens visited the capitol building.

Ensure, Insure:
Ensure means to assure; *insure* means to protect against.

■ The added step will ensure success.

■ Is your automobile adequately insured?

Farther, Further:
Farther refers to physical distance; *further* means additional.

■ Reno is farther west than Denver.

■ Do you need further information?

Fewer, Less:
Fewer refers to number; *less* refers to degree.

■ Fewer than 10 people responded.

■ It occurred less frequently than before.

Principal, Principle:
Principal means main, or first in importance, or the head of a
school; *principle* means rule.

■ The principal cause was unemployment.

■ The principal commended the fine teacher.

■ It's a matter of principle.

Some Time, Sometime, Sometimes:
Some time means a period of time; *sometime* means a vague,
unspecified time; *sometimes* means occasionally.

■ I will need some time to do my work.

■ I plan to visit Russia sometime.

■ Sometimes I wish I could be young again.

Than, Then:
Than means compared to; *then* means at that time.

■ Let's meet today rather than next week.

■ I plan to visit the project then.

5

Take a Moment

Practice using some of these frequently confused words by completing the sentences. Solutions are on page 94.

1. Capital/Capitol

What is the _____ of Pennsylvania?

2. Principal/Principle

Marietta was recently promoted to _____ of the school.

3. Some Time/Sometime/ Sometimes

_____ we forget that it requires _____ to learn to use new software.

4. Fewer/Less

Would we have _____ problems if we had _____ employees?

5. Affect/Effect

The _____ of the devastating hurricane will _____ hundreds of residents for many years.

6. Ensure/Insure

Our goal is to _____ the success of the project.

7. Than/Then

If you had been given a choice _____, would you have chosen to relocate rather _____ stay?

8. Farther/Further

How much _____ do we have to drive?

9. Accept/Except

I simply cannot _____ the job offer at that salary.

10. All Ready/Already

We are _____ past our deadline.
Are you _____ to defend our position?

Using Correct Grammar

Grammatical errors in business writing often occur in one of four categories:

1. Change in tense

2. Agreement of subject and verb

3. Agreement of pronouns and their antecedents.

4. Possessives

Understanding each of these and watching for them in your own writing will help you become a careful writer.

Changes in Tense

The mention of *tense* strikes fear in many writers—perhaps even you. This discussion will help you spot misuses of tense in your writing. Let's look at some examples.

Shift in Verb Tense

First draft:	We were balancing our books. Suddenly the lights go out.
Revision:	We were balancing our books. Suddenly the lights went out.

The verbs in the first draft shift from the past to the present tense. Both verbs in the revised sentence are in the past tense.

Shift in Voice

First draft:	You need to be aware of potential errors that keep our work from being acceptable.
Revision:	You need to be aware of potential errors that keep your work from being acceptable.
Revision:	We need to be aware of potential errors that keep our work from being acceptable.

In the first draft, the voice shifts from the second person (you) to the third person (our). Two revisions are shown; the better one is the one that conveys the intended meaning.

Agreement of Subject and Verb

The subject and verb must agree in number.

Remember this simple guideline: *The subject and verb must agree in number.* If you use a singular subject, use a singular verb. If you use a plural subject, use a plural verb.

Lack of Agreement

First draft: Each one are eligible for the award.

Revision: Each one is eligible for the award.

Your errors in agreement may not be that obvious. The following pointers will help you refine subject/verb agreement.

1. When intervening words appear between the subject and the verb, identify the simple subject.

   ■ Each one of the employees is eligible for the award.

   One is the simple, singular subject; therefore, the correct verb is the singular *is.*

2. *There* or *here* is never the subject of the sentence. Find the simple subject elsewhere in the sentence and select the verb that agrees with it.

   ■ There were 70 retirees at the annual luncheon.

   The subject is *retirees;* the plural *were* agrees with it.

3. *Each, every, many a,* and *indefinite pronouns* take singular verbs.

   ■ Many a young man wishes he had studied harder.

   ■ Everybody thrives on compliments.

   The singular verbs *wishes* and *thrives* agree with the singular subjects. When subjects are joined by *either/or* or *neither/nor,* the verb agrees with the subject closest to it.

   ■ Neither the president nor his assistants agree with the new policy.

   Assistants is nearer to the plural *agree.*

Agreement of Pronouns and Their Antecedents

Pronouns must agree with their antecedents. The *antecedent* is simply the word for which the pronoun stands. Consider the following example:

■ The technician forgot one of her important tools.

Her is the pronoun; *technician* is the antecedent.

Agreement of pronouns and antecedents must occur in two contexts:

◆ **Agreement in number:** Choose a singular pronoun for a singular antecedent; choose a plural pronoun for a plural antecedent.

◆ **Agreement in gender:** When the antecedent is specifically male or female, make sure the pronoun agrees with it. Often, the antecedent could refer to either or both sexes. Sexist references are unacceptable in today's business environment. The following examples will help you avoid this.

5

Lack of Agreement in Number

First draft:	Every one of the young women forgot their sales manuals.
Revision:	Every one of the young women forgot her sales manuals.
First draft:	Neither partner, Christina nor Josephine, wishes to give up their personal secretary.
Revision:	Neither partner, Christina nor Josephine, wishes to give up her personal secretary.

Lack of Agreement in Gender

First draft:	Each instructor will write his own evaluation.
Revision:	Each instructor will write his or her own evaluation.

Possessives

An easy-to-remember rule will help you form possessives correctly: If the word does not end in *s*, add *'s*. If the word already ends in *s*, add the apostrophe.

Words Not Ending in S	
Base word	**Possessive form**
employer	employer's
assistant	assistant's
director	director's
women	women's
day	day's

Words Ending in S	
Base word	**Possessive form**
typists	typists'
ladies	ladies'
managers	managers'
girls	girls'
weeks	weeks'

Also consider the following when forming possessives:

◆ When the base word ends in s, add 's when you pronounce the additional syllable. Add only the apostrophe if you do not pronounce the added syllable.

the actress's costume   Sears' warehouse

Gladys's new house   Ms. James' assistants

◆ Some terms are descriptive terms rather than possessives. Do not add an apostrophe to these.

the Word Processors Consortium   United States budget

American Bankers Association   Massachusetts laws

Take a Moment

You have completed a quick review of four of the language elements that need to be considered by the business writer. You can now apply what you have learned to the following sentences. Read each sentence. Correct a word or phrase, or rewrite the sentence, as appropriate. Suggested solutions are on page 94.

Change in tense:
The staff meeting began at 9 a.m. sharp; Concetta strolls in at 9:45.

_____

_____

Agreement of subject and verb:
Neither the controller nor the analyst want to change the current system.

_____

_____

Agreement of pronoun and antecedent:
The surgeon must be dedicated to his task.

_____

_____

Possessives:
When will your boss' monthly sales report be ready?

_____

_____

5

Putting It All Together

You have just reviewed the finishing touches that create successful business documents—documents that bring results. You are now ready to apply this knowledge to a sample letter.

Read the following letter. The contents of the letter are basically good. However, its effectiveness is lost in little errors. Correct them, referring to the preceding pages as necessary.

August 17, 1999

Marty Levity, Managing Director
Showtime Theatricals
4556 East 56th Street
New York, NY 09056

Dear Marty

Thanks for confirming our commitment to participate
in the December Festival of Lights. Each of our
principle performers are already to studying their
roles. Your enthusiasm has captured us to!

Its such an exciting time here. It is our privilege
to be a sponsor of the Physically Challenged
Children's Day events at Hyde Park on September 15.
I recall that you have had a keen interest in this
in the passed. Julie was speaking at our planning
session last Thursday when the lights go out. Never
a dull moment—or a blank calendar!

Everyone sends his regards. I'll in touch very
soon.

Sincerely

Esther Rabinowitz
Scheduling Director

jek

Rewrite the letter in the space provided. A suggested solution
appears on page 95.

_____

_____

_____

_____

_____

_____

_____

_____

_____

_____

_____

_____

_____

5

_____

_____

_____

_____

_____

_____

_____

_____

_____

_____

_____

Posttest

Congratulations! You have just taken another important step in your professional development by completing *Writing for Business Results.*

This posttest is provided as a quick means of reinforcing the material you have just covered. Answers are on page 95.

Approximate time to complete: 15 minutes

INSTRUCTIONS: Circle the letter of the correct answer.

1. Which of the following is a good reason for writing a business letter?
   a. To avoid conveying embarrassing information by phone.
   b. To respond to an inquiry.
   c. To prove one's worth to the employer by generating paperwork.
   d. To avoid a personal contact.

2. If you have difficulty getting started when writing, the best solution is to:
   a. Prepare a draft copy.
   b. Put it off until the end of the day after your other work is done.
   c. Begin writing.
   d. Write a final copy on your first try to make up for lost time.

3. The beginning of the letter is important because:
   a. It identifies you as the writer.
   b. Letters with dull openings seldom recover.
   c. You have four seconds to gain your reader's attention.
   d. Most people never read the last part of the letter.

4. The proper sequence for writing a letter or memo is:
   a. Plan, arrange, fill in details, and write.
   b. Plan and write.
   c. Gather details, make a plan, and write.
   d. Write individual paragraphs, arrange them in proper sequence, and rewrite.

5. Which of the following closings would be most appropriate for a sales letter?
   a. You are a phone call away from enjoying your new widget!
   b. If you want to order a widget, please call me.
   c. Widgets cost only $9.95 each.
   d. We hope you will seriously consider purchasing a widget soon.

6. The readability quotient of your letter involves:
   a. The reading level.
   b. The amount of friendliness that emanates from your writing.
   c. The overall appearance of your letter.
   d. The number of paragraphs you have used.

7. The most critical question you can ask yourself before writing is:
   a. To whom am I writing?
   b. What do I want the reader to know or do after reading this letter/memo?
   c. Who else might read this?
   d. When should I write this?

8. One of the secrets of successful memos is:
   a. Say only what is necessary.
   b. Keep the length to two or three paragraphs.
   c. Write as often as necessary until you are certain the message is understood.
   d. Write a friendly last paragraph.

9. Electronic messages differ from memos in which of the following ways?
   a. Since they are transmitted via computer, their importance is understood.
   b. The language of electronic messages is more succinct.
   c. It is never necessary to keep a hard copy.
   d. They are more personal.

10. Conciseness, one of the five Cs of business writing, is:
    a. Using long words and repeating words as necessary.
    b. Writing as briefly as possible.
    c. Eliminating excess and long words, as well as redundant expressions.
    d. Presenting all the facts.

11. You can achieve clarity in your writing by:
    a. Using jargon so the reader understands your position.
    b. Controlling the number of paragraphs.
    c. Avoiding the use of vague language and jargon.
    d. Writing very short sentences.

12. Which of the following sentences applies the write-for-results principles?
    a. At a later date, we will review our position.
    b. Thank you in advance for your cooperation.
    c. We are certain that you can never understand our position.
    d. Your concerns are our concerns.

13. A condescending tone in writing is:
    a. Sometimes necessary in order to convey the message.
    b. A matter of tone rather than words.
    c. Writing at an elementary reading level.
    d. Avoiding the use of big words.

14. Which of the following sentences is grammatically correct?
    a. Neither person, Mary or Juan, wishes to give up his secretary.
    b. Every one of the members is planning to participate.
    c. The three manager's offices are being renovated.
    d. There is a number of people who have not responded.

15. Which of the following sentences contains no spelling errors?
    a. The controller said the major capitol commitment was a positive step.
    b. Melinda Jones will supercede Richard Cruz next month.
    c. We are unable to acommodate your request at this time.
    d. Your recommendation is accepted.

Sample Letters

The following sample letters were all created in block format style, but they could also be correctly presented in modified block format style. Refer to Chapter 1 on pages 19–20 to review both styles.

- ◆ Adjustment Letter
- ◆ Inquiry Letter
- ◆ Order Letter
- ◆ Regrets Letter

Adjustment Letter

May 15, 1999

Sylvia Jordan, Manager
Madison Business Suppliers
P.O. Box 1221
Silver Spring, MD 20923

Dear Ms. Jordan

On February 28, 1999, you installed a water-
purification system in our office building. On the
following dates, we requested service: March 3, 10,
20, 25; April 7, 14, 20, 23; May 2, 9, 10. And the
system is not functioning today.

We feel that we have been more than patient with
the system and the work of your technicians. As I
said on the phone this morning, I want the system
removed immediately. Also, please issue a check for
$935.35, the amount we have paid to date.

Please complete the above transaction no later than
May 22, 1999.

Sincerely

Peter J. Pososki
President

jt

- ◆ Provide details of the original purchase or service.
- ◆ State the complaint clearly and concisely.
- ◆ State the action you wish the reader to take.

Inquiry Letter

May 15, 1999

Time Distributors
P.O. Box 355
Staten Island, NY 10325

Ladies and Gentlemen

Our publishing company is planning its annual sales
meeting on June 30, 1999, in Atlanta, Georgia.
Approximately 225 persons will attend.

While I realize the time is short, is it possible
to obtain 250 copies of your brochure "Quality Time
in Quality Lives" before June 15? These can be
shipped C.O.D. to my attention at the above
address.

If possible, would you call my assistant, Ivan
Jabobs, at 401-8785-3453, within the next week to
let him know whether these are available. Your
cooperation is very much appreciated.

Sincerely

Kazam Soroosh
Employment Relations

vc

♦ State purpose of letter by providing necessary background information.

♦ Make request.

♦ Provide all important details.

♦ Express appreciation of request response.

Order Letter

```
May 15, 1999


Quick Copy Suppliers
P.O. Box 667
Madison, WI 53710


Ladies/Gentlemen

Please send the following items to the above
address via Fast Express Next Day Air:

Quantity     Catalog No. Item          Unit Price
Total

15           675-XS      Cartridge     $105.25
$1,578.75
                         Toner 25

15 cases     2323-Q      Card Stock    $45.10
$676.50
                         Canary

Our purchase order No. 6675 is enclosed. Thank you.

Sincerely



Andrew Kim
Warehouse Inventory Specialist

bbn
```

- ◆ Give specific ordering information—make sure all information about the item is included.

- ◆ Tell how payment is to be made.

- ◆ Give shipping information.

Regrets Letter

May 15, 1999

Avran Hamani, Program Director
Greater Omaha Small Business Association
9090 Menominee Street
Omaha, NE 68125

Dear Avran

Christine Blews has asked me to express her deep
regrets that she is unable to accept your
invitation to speak at the July meeting of GOSBA.
She will be in Europe during that time.

Ms. Blews knows several members of your group and
often cites the enthusiasm and dedication of those
people.

Please extend your invitation again. Due to her
busy schedule, I suggest a lead time of six months,
if your planning permits.

Sincerely

Marty Goebel
Secretary to Christine Blews

mtr

- ◆ Express regrets in the first paragraph.

- ◆ When appropriate, give reasons for a decision.

- ◆ Close with a statement of goodwill.

Answers to Selected Exercises

Chapter One

Take a Moment (page 10)

Why was the letter written?
> To inform

How well do you think the writer knows the reader?
> Not at all

Does the letter convey a warm, human element?
> Yes

What information was necessary?
> Invitation to speaker
> Audience, date, time, and place
> Information for response

What result does the writer want?
> A positive response to the invitation

Take a Moment (page 12)

List the major points to be covered:
1. Purpose for writing
2. Verification of date, time, place, event
3. Formal request to place in file

Putting It All Together (page 21)

Letter Plan:
1. Thank-you
2. Information on product
3. Possible follow-through at later date

Suggested Letter (page 22)

Thank you for your inquiry regarding Version 2.1 of
RapidWrite software.

The projected delivery date of V.2 1 is first
quarter, 1999. While pricing information is not
available at this time, we do not anticipate any
major increases. Of course, experienced users like
you will be able to upgrade from V.2.0 at a minimal
cost.

You will be pleased to know that V.2.1 will include
many of the enhancements suggested by our current
users. Please continue to call our technical
assistants at 1-800-225-5000 whenever you have a
question or suggestion. Each one is important to us
and is considered for future upgrades.

Chapter Two

Take a Moment (page 30)

List the major points to be covered.
1. The three new mailing deadlines
2. Effective date

Putting It All Together (page 34)

Memo-writing plan:
1. Details of presentation
2. Notice to bring 12 copies of five-year department plans

Suggested Memo (page 35)

The preliminary architectural plans for our
expansion will be presented by Letitia Villacorta on
Tuesday, March 15, at 9 a.m. in my office.

Please bring 12 copies of your five-year department
plans for distribution.

Chapter Three

Take a Moment (page 47)

Conciseness
Too many employees are taking extended coffee and lunch breaks.
Completeness
Your performance review will be August 9 at 9:30 a.m. in Personnel A-25.
Courtesy
When a good customer like you misses a payment, I know something is wrong.
Clarity
A review of your substance-abuse program will be conducted by members of UNLV's Wellness Division.
Correctness
Four months have only 30 days: April, June, September, and November.

Putting It All Together (page 51)

```
February 1, 1999


Martin G. LeFavre
3301 Eastern Ave., Apt. 211
Wichita, KS 67215

Dear Martin

Thank you for applying for a sales position in our
company. Unfortunately, we do not have any openings at
this time.

Your file will remain active for a period of six months.
If you wish to submit another application at that time,
please send it to the attention of Kathryn O'Connor,
Director of Human Resources.

Good luck in your job search!

Sincerely
```

Chapter Four

Take a Moment (page 58)

Use as few words as possible:
> The current balance on your account is $259.95.

Eliminate redundant expressions:
> In my opinion, the attached statement contains the facts in the case.

Use positive words and phrases:
> The enclosed brochure will help you understand why prompt payments are important.

Eliminate clichés and jargon:
> Thank you for helping us set our priorities.

Avoid sexist references:
> Employees hold their future within their own hands.

Take a Moment (page 62)

Use active verbs:
> The new vacation policy, approved by the employee task force, gives employees with five or more years of service one additional week of vacation.

Avoid a condescending tone:
> We continue to maintain our policy of payment due upon delivery, unless prior arrangements have been made.

Use simple words:
> Enclosed is a copy of Act #563 giving Kansas City homeowners the right to appeal property tax rates.

Take a Moment (page 65)

Consider the interests of the reader:

Please indicate on the enclosed postal card the color and size of the file cabinet you wish, and we will process your order immediately.

Pay attention to details:

Each of the divisions has made a firm commitment to better quality control.

Putting It All Together (page 67)

```
February 20, 1999

Ara Godosian, Manager
ABC Suppliers Inc.
P.O. Box 4857
Newark, NJ 07152

Dear Mr. Godosian

Our records indicate that your account has been past
due for five of the last six months. For that reason,
all future sales must be on a cash basis.

You have been a good customer of long standing, and I
am sorry to have to take this action. Because you and
I have had an excellent business relationship, I have
been granted one deviation from our company policy:
Your credit account will be kept open for the next 10
days. If you wish to appeal our action, you may do so
within that time frame.

Sincerely


Patrick Monaghan
Controller
```

Chapter Five

Take a Moment (page 72)

1. What is the capital of Pennsylvania?

2. Marietta was recently promoted to principal of the school.

3. Sometimes we forget that it requires some time to learn to use new software.

4. Would we have fewer problems if we had fewer employees?

5. The effect of the devastating hurricane will affect hundreds of residents for many years.

6. Our goal is to ensure the success of the project.

7. If you had been given a choice then, would you have chosen to relocate rather than to stay?

8. How much farther do we have to drive?

9. I simply cannot accept the job offer at that salary.

10. We are already past our deadline. Are you all ready to defend our position?

Take a Moment (page 77)

Change in tense:
> The staff meeting began at 9 a.m. sharp; Concetta strolled in at 9:45.

Agreement of subject and verb:
> Neither the controller nor the analyst wants to change the current system.

Agreement of pronoun and antecedent:
> Surgeons must be dedicated to their task.

Possessives:
> When will your boss's monthly sales report be ready?

Putting It All Together (page 79)

```
August 17, 1999

Marty Levity, Managing Director
Showtime Theatricals
4556 East 56th Street
New York, NY 09056

Dear Marty

Thanks for confirming our commitment to participate
in the December Festival of Lights. All of our
principal performers are already studying their
roles. Your enthusiasm has captured us too!

It's such an exciting time here. It is our privilege
to be a sponsor of the Physically Challenged
Children's Day events at Hyde Park on September 15.
I recall that you have had a keen interest in this
in the past. Julie was speaking at our planning
session last Thursday when the lights went out.
Never a dull moment—or a blank calendar!

Everyone sends regards. I'll be in touch very soon.

Sincerely


Esther Rabinowitz
Scheduling Director

jek
```

Posttest (pages 80—83)

1. b	6. a	11. c
2. c	7. a	12. a
3. b	8. a	13. b
4. a	9. b	14. b
5. a	10. c	15. d

Skill Maintenance

You'll get the most out of the training you've just completed if you reinforce your skills at regular intervals. This Skill Maintenance checklist will help you practice and maintain your skills.

Write today's date _____.

Using this date as a base, fill in the three dates on top of the columns at the right. Put a reminder on your calendar to return to this checklist on those dates. Refer to a letter or memo you've written recently, and complete the following checklist. Use the chapter reference column to review the principle of effective writing for any item checked "No."

	Date_____ 3 months		Date_____ 6 months		Date_____ 1 year		Chapter Reference
	Yes	No	Yes	No	Yes	No	
1. I prepared a plan before I wrote.							1, 2
2. I wrote a draft before I wrote the final copy.							1, 2
3. My opening is a grabber.							1, 2
4. My main message contains all the necessary information for the reader to take action of respond.							1, 2
5. I have indicated what action or results I am seeking.							1
6. My closing wraps up my writing.							1, 2
7. My format is consistent with generally accepted or corporate practices.							1, 2
8. I can identify the five Cs in my writing: conciseness, completeness, courtesy, clarity, and correctness.							3
9. I use the write-for-results principles in all my writing.							4
10. My spelling and grammar are correct in every detail.							5